— The Complete —
Life's Little Instruction Book®

"The Flodmas"

"HAPPY B-DAY Mike"

"JAN. 20 2008"

— The Complete —
Life's Little Instruction Book®

H. Jackson Brown, Jr.

Published by
THOMAS NELSON
Since 1798

www.thomasnelson.com

Published in Nashville, Tennessee, by Thomas Nelson, Inc.

Art Direction & Design by Mary Hooper

Library of Congress Cataloging-in-Publication Data

Brown, H. Jackson, 1940–

   [Life's little instruction book]
   The complete life's little instruction book / H. Jackson Brown, Jr.
   p. cm.
   Originally published in 3 vols. : Life's little instruction book.
   Nashville, Tenn. : Rutledge Hill Press, c1991–c1995.
   ISBN 1-4016-0332-7
   1. Happiness—Quotations, maxims, etc. 2. Conduct of life—
   Quotations, maxims, etc. I. Title.
   [BJ1481.B87 1997]
   170'.44—dc21   97-5575
                                              CIP

Printed in Canada

07 08 09 10 – 6 5 4 3 2 1

INTRODUCTION

A lot has happened since the fall of 1990 when I sat at our kitchen table and jotted down a few pages of instructions and personal observations for my son, Adam. He was beginning his freshman year at college, and I felt that a collection of the insights and discoveries which had positively influenced my own life might be an appropriate gift to commemorate this important event.

As a young adult, Adam would soon find himself standing at life's most challenging crossroads. His choosing the right path would make all the difference. Here was my attempt to help his heart as well as his head to know the way.

That first list of fatherly advice contained 511 entries, and I mailed him a new collection every two years. These lists were published as three little books, and to my surprise and delight became bestsellers.

But Adam and I are most proud of the fact that this correspondence between us is available in 33 languages and, in this new format, will continue to encourage, inspire, and challenge readers throughout the world.

H. J. B.
Tall Pine Lodge
Fernvale, Tennessee

For Adam, my son
and in many ways, my teacher.

Son, how can I help you see?
May I give you my shoulders to stand on?
Now you see farther than me.
Now you see for both of us.
Won't you tell me what you see?

Other Books by H. Jackson Brown, Jr.

Life's Little Instruction Book®
(volumes I, II, and III)

Live and Learn and Pass It On
(volumes I, II, and III)

Complete Live and Learn and Pass It On

Highlighted in Yellow
(with Rochelle Pennington)

Volume I

1. Compliment three people every day.

2. Have a dog.

3. Watch a sunrise at least once a year.

4. Remember other people's birthdays.

5. Overtip breakfast waitresses.

6. Have a firm handshake.

7. Hug children after you discipline them.

8. Look people in the eye.

9. Say "thank you" a lot.

10. Say "please" a lot.

11. Learn to play a musical instrument.

12. Sing in the shower.

13. Use the good silver.

14. Buy great books, even if you never read them.

15. Learn to make great chili.

16. Plant flowers every spring.

17. Own a great sound system.

18. Be the first to say, "Hello."

19. Live beneath your means.

20. Drive inexpensive cars, but own the best house you can afford.

21. Be forgiving of yourself and others.

22. Learn three clean jokes.

23. Wear polished shoes.

24. Floss your teeth.

25. Drink champagne for no reason at all.

26. Ask for a raise when you feel you've earned it.

27. If in a fight, hit first and hit hard.

28. Return all the things you borrow.

The Complete Life's Little Instruction Book

29. Teach some kind of class.

30. Be a student in some kind of class.

31. Never buy a house without a fireplace.

32. Buy whatever kids are selling on card tables in their front yard.

33. Once in your life own a convertible.

34. Plant a tree on your birthday.

35. Donate two pints of blood every year.

36. Treat everyone you meet like you want to be treated.

37. Learn to identify the music of Chopin, Mozart, and Beethoven.

38. Make new friends but cherish the old ones.

39. Keep secrets.

40. Take lots of snapshots.

41. Never refuse homemade brownies.

42. Don't postpone joy.

43. Write "thank you" notes promptly.

44. Show respect for teachers.

45. Show respect for police officers and firefighters.

46. Show respect for military personnel.

47. Don't waste time learning the "tricks of the trade." Instead, learn the trade.

48. Never give up
on anybody.
Miracles happen
every day.

49. Keep a tight rein on your temper.

50. Buy vegetables from truck farmers who advertise with hand-lettered signs.

51. Put the cap back on the toothpaste.

52. Take out the garbage without being told.

53. Avoid overexposure to the sun.

54. Vote.

55. Surprise loved ones with little unexpected gifts.

56. Stop blaming others. Take responsibility for every area of your life.

57. Never mention being on a diet.

58. Make the best of bad situations.

59. Live so that when your children think of fairness, caring, and integrity, they think of you.

60. Support a high school band.

61. Admit your mistakes.

62. Ask someone to pick up your mail and daily paper when you're out of town. Those are the first two things potential burglars look for.

63. Use your wit to amuse, not abuse.

64. Remember that all news is biased.

65. Take a photography course.

66. Be brave. Even if you're not, pretend to be. No one can tell the difference.

67. Let people pull in front of you when you're stopped in traffic.

68. Always accept an outstretched hand.

69. Demand excellence and be willing to pay for it.

70. Whistle.

71. Give to charity all the clothes you haven't worn during the past three years.

72. Learn to make something beautiful with your hands.

73. Never forget your anniversary.

74. Eat prunes.

75. Ride a bike.

76. Choose a charity in your community and support it generously with your time and money.

77. Don't take good health for granted.

78. When someone wants to hire you, even if it's for a job you have little interest in, talk to them. Never close the door on an opportunity until you've had a chance to hear the offer in person.

79. Don't mess with drugs, and don't associate with those who do.

80. Slow dance.

81. Steer clear of restaurants with strolling musicians.

82. Avoid sarcastic remarks.

83. Forget the Joneses.

84. When you want to teach a lesson, tell a story.

85. Even if you're financially well-to-do, have your children earn and pay for all their automobile insurance.

86. Even if you're financially well-to-do, have your children earn and pay part of their college tuition.

87. In business and in family relationships, remember that the most important thing is trust.

88. Don't smoke.

89. Refill ice cube trays.

90. Don't let anyone ever see you tipsy.

91. Become knowledgeable about antiques, oriental rugs, and contemporary art.

92. Recycle old newspapers, bottles, and cans.

93. Never invest more in the stock market than you can afford to lose.

94. Make it a habit to do nice things for people who'll never find it out.

95. Attend class reunions.

96. Always have something beautiful in sight, even if it's just a daisy in a jelly glass.

97. # Think big thoughts, but relish small pleasures.

98. Lend only those books you never care to see again.

99. Never start a business with someone who has more troubles than you.

100. Read the Bill of Rights.

101. Learn how to read a financial report.

102. Tell your kids often how terrific they are and that you trust them.

103. Never cheat.

The Complete Life's Little Instruction Book

104. Use credit cards only for convenience, never for credit.

105. Treat yourself to a massage on your birthday.

106. Take a brisk thirty-minute walk every day.

107. When dining with clients or business associates, never order more than one cocktail or one glass of wine. If no one else is drinking, don't drink at all.

108. Smile a lot. It costs nothing and is beyond price.

109. Know how to drive a stick shift.

110. Spread crunchy peanut butter on Pepperidge Farm Gingerman cookies for the perfect late-night snack.

111. Never use profanity.

112. Never argue with police officers, and address them as "officer."

113. Learn to identify local wildflowers, birds, and trees.

114. Keep a fire extinguisher in your kitchen and car.

115. Respect your children's privacy. Knock before entering their room.

116. Install dead bolt locks on outside doors.

117. Don't buy expensive wine, luggage, or watches.

118. Consider writing a living will.

119. Put a lot of little marshmallows in your hot chocolate.

120. Learn CPR.

121. Resist the temptation to buy a boat.

122. Stop and read historical roadside markers.

123. Give yourself a year and read the Bible cover to cover.

124. Learn to listen. Opportunity sometimes knocks very softly.

125. Know how to change a tire.

126. Know how to tie a bow tie.

127. Wear audacious underwear under the most solemn business attire.

128. Remember people's names.

129. Introduce yourself to the manager where you bank. It's important that he or she knows you personally.

130. Learn the capitals of the states.

131. Visit Washington, D.C., and do the tourist bit.

132. Leave the toilet seat in the down position.

133. When someone is relating an important event that's happened to them, don't try to top them with a story of your own. Let them have the stage.

134. Have crooked teeth straightened.

135. Have dull-colored teeth whitened.

136. Keep your watch five minutes fast.

137. Learn Spanish. In a few years, more than thirty-five percent of all Americans will speak it as their first language.

138. When starting out, don't worry about not having enough money. Limited funds are a blessing, not a curse. Nothing encourages creative thinking in quite the same way.

139. Pay your bills on time.

140. Never deprive someone of hope; it might be all they have.

141. Don't buy cheap tools. Craftsman tools from Sears are among the best.

142. Give yourself an hour to cool off before responding to someone who has provoked you. If it involves something really important, give yourself overnight.

143. Join a slow-pitch softball league.

144. Keep a flashlight and extra batteries under the bed and in the glove box of your car.

145. Take someone bowling.

146. When playing games with children, let them win.

147. Turn off the television at dinner time.

148. Learn to handle a pistol and rifle safely.

149. Skip one meal a week and give what you would have spent to a street person.

150. Sing in a choir.

151. Get acquainted with a good lawyer, accountant, and plumber.

152. Fly Old Glory on the Fourth of July.

153. Stand at attention and put your hand over your heart when singing the national anthem.

154. Resist the temptation to put a cute message on your answering machine.

155. Have a will and tell your next-of-kin where it is.

156. Have regular medical and dental checkups.

157. Take time to smell the roses.

158. Be tough minded but tenderhearted.

159. Pray not for things, but for wisdom and courage.

160. Use seat belts.

161. Strive for excellence, not perfection.

162. Keep your desk and work area neat.

163. Take an overnight train trip and sleep in a Pullman.

164. Avoid negative people.

165. Resist telling people how something should be done. Instead, tell them what needs to be done. They will often surprise you with creative solutions.

166. Don't waste time responding to your critics.

167. Don't scrimp in order to leave money to your children.

168. Be original.

169. Be neat.

170. Never give up on what your really want to do. The person with big dreams is more powerful than one with all the facts.

171. Be punctual and insit on it in others.

172. Be suspicious of all politicians.

173. Encourage your children to have a part-time job after the age of sixteen.

174. Never take action when you're angry.

175. Read carefully anything that requires your signature. Remember the big print giveth and the small print taketh away.

176. **Be kinder than necessary.**

177. Give people a second chance, but not a third.

178. When you're proud of your children, let them know it.

179. Be your wife's best friend.

180. Do battle against prejudice and discrimination wherever you find it.

181. Wear out, don't rust out.

182. Be romantic.

183. Let people know what you stand for—and what you won't stand for.

184. Don't forget, a person's greatest emotional need is to feel appreciated.

185. Never criticize the person who signs your paycheck. If you are unhappy with your job, find another one .

186. Be insatiably curious. Ask "why" a lot.

187. Learn how to fix a leaky faucet and toilet.

188. Become the
most positive
and enthusiastic
person you know.

189. Measure people by the size of their hearts, not the size of their bank accounts.

190. Have good posture. Enter a room with purpose and confidence.

191. Observe the speed limit.

192. Drink low fat milk.

193. Use less salt.

194. Eat less red meat.

195. Don't worry that you can't give your kids the best of everything. Give them your very best.

196. Determine the quality of a neighborhood by the manners of the people living there.

197. Don't quit a job until you've lined up another.

198. Park at the back of the lot at shopping centers. The walk is good exercise.

199. Surprise a new neighbor with one of your favorite homemade dishes— and include the recipe.

200. Ask your boss who his or her heroes are.

201. Don't watch violent television shows, and don't buy the products that sponsor them.

202. Don't carry a grudge.

203. Show respect for all living things.

204. Return borrowed vehicles with the gas tank full.

205. Choose work that is in harmony with your values.

206. Loosen up. Relax. Except for rare life-and-death matters, nothing is as important as it seems.

207. Swing for the fence.

208. Attend high school art shows, and always buy something.

209. Give your best to your employer.
It's one of the best investments you
can make.

210. Take your dog to obedience school.
You'll both learn a lot.

211. Don't allow the phone to interupt
important moments. It's there for
your convenience, not the caller's.

212. Don't waste time grieving over
past mistakes. Learn from them
and move on.

213. Commit yourself to constant self-improvement.

214. When complimented, a sincere "thank you" is the only response required.

215. Don't plan a long evening on a blind date. A lunch date is perfect. If things don't work out, both of you have wasted only an hour.

216. Don't discuss business in elevators or restrooms. You never know who may overhear you.

217. Have impeccable manners.

218. Be a good loser.

219. Be a good winner.

220. Never go grocery shopping when you're hungry. You'll buy too much.

221. Spend less time worrying who's right, and more time deciding what's right.

222. Praise in public.

223. Criticize in private.

224. Don't major in
minor things.

225. Think twice before burdening a friend with a secret.

226. Never tell anyone they look tired or depressed.

227. When someone hugs you, let them be the first to let go.

228. Resist giving advice concerning matrimony, finances, or hair styles.

229. Never pay for work before it's completed.

230. Keep good company.

231. Keep a daily journal.

232. Keep your promises.

233. Teach your children the value of
money and the importance of saving.

234. Be willing to lose a battle in order
to win the war.

235. Don't be deceived by first
impressions.

236. Avoid any church that has cushions on the pews and is considering building a gymnasium.

237. Seek out the good in people.

238. Don't encourage rude or inattentive service by tipping the standard amount.

239. Watch the movie *It's a Wonderful Life* every Christmas.

240. Respect tradition.

241. Never cut what can be untied.

242. Drink eight glasses of water every day.

243. Be cautious about lending money to a friend. You might lose both.

244. Never waste an opportunity to tell good employees how much they mean to the company.

245. Wave at children on school buses.

246. Be modest. A lot was accomplished before you were born.

247. Buy a bird feeder and hang it so that you can see it from your kitchen window.

248. Make a video of your parents' memories of how they met and their first years of marriage.

249. Show respect for others' time. Call whenever you're going to be more than five minutes late for an appointment.

250. Hire people smarter than you.

251. Learn to show cheerfulness, even when you don't feel like it.

252. Learn to show enthusiasm, even when you don't feel like it.

253. Take good care of those you love.

254. Keep it simple.

255. Never ask a lawyer or accountant for business advice. They are trained to find problems, not solutions.

256. Purchase gas from the neighborhood gas station even if it costs more. Next winter when it's six degrees and your car won't start, you'll be glad they know you.

257. Don't jaywalk.

258. When meeting someone for the first time, resist asking what they do for a living. Enjoy their company without attaching any labels.

259. Avoid like the plague any lawsuit.

260. Take family vacations whether
     you can afford them or not. The
     memories will be priceless.

261. Don't gossip.

262. Don't discuss salaries.

263. Don't nag.

264. Don't gamble.

265. Beware of the person who has
     nothing to lose.

266. Every day show your family how much you love them with your words, with your touch, and with your thoughtfulness.

267. Lie on your back and look at the stars.

268. Don't leave car keys in the ignition.

269. Don't whine.

270. Arrive at work early and stay beyond quitting time.

271. Leave everything
a little better
than you found it.

272. When facing a difficult task, act as though it is impossible to fail. If you're going after Moby Dick, take along the tartar sauce.

273. Change air conditioner filters every three months.

274. Cut out complimentary newspaper articles about people you know and mail the articles to them with notes of congratulations.

275. Never overstay your welcome.

276. Remember that overnight success usually takes about fifteen years.

277. Fill your gas tank when it falls below one-quarter full.

278. Don't expect money to bring you happiness.

279. Never snap your fingers to get someone's attention. It's rude.

280. No matter how dire the situation, keep your cool.

281. When paying cash, ask for a discount.

282. Find a good tailor.

283. Don't use a toothpick in public.

284. Never underestimate your power to change yourself.

285. Never overestimate your power to change others.

286. Promise big. Deliver big.

287. Practice empathy. Try to see things from other people's point of view.

288. Discipline yourself to save money. It's essential to success.

289. Get and stay in shape.

290. Find some other way of proving your manhood than by shooting defenseless animals and birds.

291. Remember the deal's not done until the check has cleared the bank.

292. Don't spread yourself too thin.
     Learn to say no politely and quickly.

293. Keep overhead low.

294. Keep expectations high.

295. Accept pain and disappointment
     as part of life.

296. Remember that a successful
     marriage depends on two things:
     (1) finding the right person and
     (2) being the right person.

297. Don't burn bridges. You'll be surprised how many times you have to cross the same river.

298. See problems as opportunities for growth and self-mastery.

299. Don't believe people when they ask you to be honest with them.

300. Don't expect life to be fair.

301. Remember that enough is better than too much.

302. Lock your car even if it's parked in your own driveway.

303. Never go to bed with dirty dishes in the sink.

304. Learn to handle a handsaw and a hammer.

305. Compliment the meal when you're a guest in someone's home.

306. Make the bed when you're an overnight visitor in someone's home.

307. Judge your success by the degree that you're enjoying peace, health, and love.

308. Take a nap on Sunday afternoons.

309. Contribute five percent of your
      income to charity.

310. When tempted to criticize your
      parents, spouse, or children, bite
      your tongue.

311. Never underestimate the power of
      love.

312. Never underestimate the power
      of forgiveness.

313. Don't leave a ring in the bathtub.

314. Never buy dark colored sheets or towels.

315. Don't bore people with your problems. When someone asks you how you feel—say, "Terrific, never better." When they ask, "How's business?" reply, "Excellent, and getting better every day."

316. Learn to disagree without being disagreeable.

317. Be tactful. Never alienate anyone on purpose.

318. Hear both sides before judging.

319. Refrain from envy. It's the source of much unhappiness.

320. Be courteous to everyone.

321. Wave to crosswalk patrol mothers.

322. When there's no time for a full work-out, do push-ups.

323. Rekindle old friendships.

324. Don't delay acting on a good idea. Chances are someone else has just thought of it, too. Success comes to the one who acts first.

325. Don't say you don't have enough time. You have exactly the same number of hours per day that were given to Helen Keller, Pasteur, Michelangelo, Mother Teresa, Leonardo da Vinci, Thomas Jefferson, and Albert Einstein.

326. Remember that winners do what losers don't want to do.

327. Seek opportunity, not security. A boat in a harbor is safe, but in time its bottom rots out.

328. Instead of using the words *if only,* try substituting the words *next time.*

329. Instead of using the word *problem,* try substituting the word *opportunity.*

330. Every so often push your luck.

331. Live your life as
an exclamation,
not an explanation.

332. When traveling, put a card in your wallet with your name, home phone, the phone number of a friend or close relative, important medical information, plus the phone number of the hotel or motel where you're staying.

333. When you arrive at your job in the morning, let the first thing you say brighten everyone's day.

334. When renting a car for a couple of days, splurge and get the one you would someday like to own.

335. Be wary of people who tell you how honest they are.

336. Install smoke detectors in your home.

337. Get your next pet from the animal shelter.

338. Live your life so that your epitaph could read, "No regrets."

339. Never walk out on a quarrel with your wife.

340. Reread your favorite book.

341. Don't be fooled. If something sounds too good to be true, it probably is.

342. Regarding furniture and clothes: if you think you'll be using them five years or longer, buy the best you can afford.

343. Be bold and courageous. When you look back on your life, you'll regret the things you didn't do more than the ones you did.

344. Patronize drug stores with soda fountains.

345. Try everything offered by supermarket food demonstrators.

346. Own a good dictionary.

347. Own a good thesaurus.

348. Go through all your old photographs. Select ten and tape them to your kitchen cabinets. Change them every thirty days.

349. Remember the three most important things when buying a home: location, location, location.

350. Keep valuable papers in a bank lockbox.

351. Just for fun, attend a small town Fourth of July celebration.

352. To explain a romantic break-up, simply say, "It was all my fault."

353. Be there when people need you.

354. Never waste an opportunity to tell someone you love them.

355. Evaluate yourself by your own standards, not someone else's.

356. Let your representatives in Washington know how you feel. Call (202) 225-3121 for the House and (202) 224-3121 for the Senate. An operator will connect you to the right office.

357. Be decisive even if it means you'll sometimes be wrong.

358. Be prepared to lose once in a while.

359. Don't let anyone talk you out of pursuing what you know to be a great idea.

360. Never eat the last cookie.

361. Every day look for some small way to improve your marriage.

362. Every day look for some small way to improve the way you do your job.

363. Don't flush urinals with your hand— use your elbow.

364. Acquire things the old-fashioned way: Save for them and pay cash.

365. Know when to keep silent.

366. Know when to speak up.

367. Remember no one makes it alone. Have a grateful heart and be quick to acknowledge those who help you.

368. If you have an interest in the Civil War, read Winston Groom's *Shrouds of Glory* (Pocket Books, 1996).

369. Do business with those who do business with you.

370. Just to see how it feels, for the next twenty-four hours refrain from criticizing anybody or anything.

371. Give your clients your enthusiastic best.

372. Work hard to create in your children a good self-image. It's the most important thing you can do to insure their success.

373. Take charge of your attitude. Don't let someone else choose it for you.

374. Let your children overhear you saying complimentary things about them to other adults.

375. Save an evening a week for just you and your wife.

376. Carry jumper cables in your car.

377. Get all repair estimates in writing.

378. Forget committees. New, noble, world-changing ideas always come from one person working alone.

379. Pay attention to the details.

380. Be a self-starter.

381. Be loyal.

382. Understand that happiness is not based on possessions, power, or prestige, but on relationships with people you love and respect.

383. When undecided about what color to paint a room, choose antique white.

384. Never give a loved one a gift that suggests they need improvement.

385. Compliment even small improvements.

386. Turn off the tap when brushing your teeth.

387. Wear expensive shoes, belts, and ties, but buy them on sale.

388. Start meetings on time regardless of who's missing.

389. Carry stamps in your wallet. You never know when you'll discover the perfect card for a friend or loved one.

390. Street musicians are a treasure. Stop for a moment and listen; then leave a small donation.

391. Don't ever watch hot dogs or sausage being made.

392. When faced with a serious health problem, get at least three medical opinions.

393. Support equal pay for equal work.

394. Pay your fair share.

395. Remain open, flexible, and curious.

396. Never give anyone a fruitcake.

397. Never acquire just one kitten. Two are a lot more fun and no more trouble.

398. If you're going to be weird, be confident about it.

The Complete Life's Little Instruction Book

399. Stay out of nightclubs.

400. Begin each day with your favorite music.

401. Visit your city's night court on a Saturday night.

402. When attending meetings, sit down front.

403. Don't be intimidated by doctors and nurses. Even when you're in the hospital, it's still your body.

404. Focus on making things better, not bigger.

405. Read hospital bills carefully. It's reported that 89 percent contain errors—in favor of the hospital.

406. Every once in a while, take the scenic route.

407. Don't let your possessions possess you.

408. Wage war against littering.

409. Don't flaunt your success, but don't apologize for it either.

410. Send a lot of Valentine cards.
Sign them, "Someone who thinks
you're terrific."

411. Cut your own firewood.

412. When you and your wife have a
disagreement, regardless of who's
wrong, apologize. Say, "I'm sorry I
upset you. Would you forgive me?"
These are healing, magical words.

413. Be enthusiastic about the success
of others.

414. After experiencing inferior service, food, or products, bring it to the attention of the person in charge. Good managers will appreciate knowing.

415. Don't procrastinate. Do what needs doing when it needs to be done.

416. Read to your children.

417. Sing to your children.

418. Listen to your children.

419. Get your priorities straight. No one ever said on his death bed, "Gee, if I'd only spent more time at the office."

420. Turn on your headlights when it begins to rain.

421. Don't allow self-pity. The moment this emotion strikes, do something nice for someone less fortunate than you.

422. Don't accept "good enough" as good enough.

423. Take care of your reputation. It's your most valuable asset.

424. Don't tailgate.

425. Sign and carry your organ donor card.

426. Share the credit.

427. Do more than is expected

428. Go to a county fair and check out the 4-H Club exhibits. It will renew your faith in the younger generation.

429. Select a doctor your own age so that you can grow old together.

430. Have a friend who owns a truck.

431. When a guest, don't let anyone see you go back more than twice for the peeled shrimp.

432. Improve your performance by improving your attitude.

433. At the movies, buy Junior Mints and sprinkle them on your popcorn.

434. Have some knowledge of three religions other than your own.

435. Make a list of ten things you want to experience before you die. Carry it in your wallet and refer to it often.

436. Answer the phone with enthusiasm and energy in your voice.

437. Every person that you meet knows something you don't; learn from them.

438. Never put a candy dish next to the phone.

439. Tape record your parents' laughter.

440. When meeting someone you don't know well, extend your hand and give them your name. Never assume they remember you even if you've met them before.

441. Do it right the first time.

442. Laugh a lot. A good sense of humor cures almost all of life's ills.

443. Never compromise your integrity.

444. Never underestimate the power of a kind word or deed.

445. Don't undertip the waiter just because the food is bad; he didn't cook it.

446. Change your car's oil and filter every three thousand miles regardless of what the owner's manual recommends.

447. Conduct family fire drills. Be sure everyone knows what to do in case the house catches fire.

448. Be open to new ideas.

449. Don't be afraid to say, "I don't know."

450. Don't be afraid to say, "I made a mistake."

451. Don't be afraid to say, "I need help."

452. Don't be afraid to say, "I'm sorry."

453. Get organized. If you don't know where to start, read Stephanie Winston's *Getting Organized* (Warner Books, 2006).

454. Keep a note pad and pencil on your bedside table. Million-dollar ideas sometimes strike at 3 a.m.

455. Show respect for everyone who works for a living, regardless of how trivial their job.

456. When you find a job that's ideal, take it regardless of the pay. If you've got what it takes, your salary will soon reflect your value to the company.

457. Read the Sunday *New York Times* to keep informed.

458. Send your loved one flowers. Think of a reason later.

459. Attend your children's athletic contests, plays, and recitals.

460. Look for opportunities to make people feel important.

461. Don't miss the magic of the moment by focusing on what's to come.

462. Don't use time or words carelessly. Neither can be retrieved.

463. When a child falls and skins a knee or elbow, always show concern; then take the time to "kiss it and make it well."

464. When talking to the press, remember they always have the last word.

465. Set short-term and long-term goals.

466. When planning a trip abroad, read about the places you'll visit before you go or, better yet, rent a travel video.

467. Don't rain on other people's parades.

468. Stand when greeting a visitor to your office.

469. Don't interrupt.

470. Enjoy real maple syrup.

471. Don't be rushed into making an important decision. People will understand if you say, "I'd like a little more time to think it over. Can I get back to you tomorrow?"

472. Before leaving to meet a flight, call the airline first to be sure it's on time.

473. Be prepared. You never get a second chance to make a good first impression.

474. Don't expect others to listen to your advice and ignore your example.

475. Get into the habit of putting your billfold and car keys in the same place when entering your home.

476. Go the distance. When you accept
a task, finish it.

477. Give thanks before every meal.

478. Don't insist on running someone
else's life.

479. Respond promptly to R.S.V.P. invitations.
If there's a phone number, call; if not,
write a note.

480. Never admit at work that you're
tired, angry, or bored.

481. Learn a card trick.

482. Steer clear of restaurants that rotate.

483. Give people the benefit of the doubt.

484. Decide to get up thirty minutes earlier. Do this for a year, and you will add seven and one-half days to your waking world.

485. Patronize local merchants even if it costs a bit more.

486. Watch for big problems. They disguise big opportunities.

487. Take a kid to the zoo.

488. Make someone's day by paying the toll for the person in the car behind you.

489. Don't make the same mistake twice.

490. Don't drive on slick tires.

491. Save ten percent of what you earn.

492. Don't be called out on strikes. Go down swinging.

493. Keep an extra key hidden somewhere on your car in case you lock yourself out.

494. Never discuss money with people who have much more or much less than you.

495. Never buy a beige car.

496. Never buy something you don't need just because it's on sale.

497. Keep several irons in the fire.

498. Don't think a higher price always means higher quality.

499. Cherish your children for what they are, not for what you'd like them to be.

500. When negotiating your salary, think of what you want; then ask for ten percent more.

501. Be a leader: Remember the lead sled dog is the only one with a decent view.

502. Question your goals by asking, "Will this help me become my very best?"

503. Be alert for opportunities to show praise and appreciation.

504. Commit yourself to quality.

505. Your mind can only hold one thought at a time. Make it a positive and constructive one.

506. After you've worked hard to get what you want, take the time to enjoy it.

507. Never underestimate the power of words to heal and reconcile relationships.

508. Become someone's hero.

509. Marry only for love.

510. Count your blessings.

511. Call your mother.

Volume II

512. Believe in love at first sight.

513. Never laugh at anyone's dreams.

514. Overpay good baby sitters.

515. Never refuse jury duty. It is your civic responsibility, plus you'll learn a lot.

516. Accept a breath mint if someone offers you one.

517. When you feel terrific, notify your face.

518. Love deeply and passionately. You might get hurt, but it's the only way to live life completely.

519. Never apologize for being early for an appointment.

520. Open the car door for your wife and always help her with her coat.

521. Discipline with a gentle hand.

522. Look for ways to make your boss look good.

523. When reconvening after a conference break, choose a chair in a different part of the room.

524. Rake a big pile of leaves every fall and jump in it with someone you love.

525. Volunteer. Sometimes the jobs no one wants conceal big opportunities.

526. Create a little signal only your wife knows so that you can show her you love her across a crowded room.

527. Never drive while holding a cup of hot coffee between your knees.

528. Carry Handi-Wipes in your glove compartment.

529. Never miss an opportunity to ride a roller coaster.

530. Never miss an opportunity to have someone rub your back.

531. Never miss an opportunity to sleep on a screened-in porch.

532. Accept your share of hard work;
     that's where opportunities hide.

533. Have a professional photo of yourself
     made. Update it every three years.

534. Drive as you wish your kids would.
     Never speed or drive recklessly with
     children in the car.

535. Remember the advice of our friend
     Ken Beck: When you see a box turtle
     crossing the road, stop and put it
     safely on the other side.

536. Never be the first to break a family tradition.

537. Park next to the end curb in parking lots. Your car doors will have half the chance of getting dented.

538. Keep a diary of your accomplishments at work. Then when you ask for a raise, you'll have the information you need to back it up.

539. Never sign contracts with blank spaces.

540. Sign all warranty cards and mail them in promptly.

541. In disagreements, fight fairly. No name calling.

542. Never take the last piece of fried chicken.

543. When you go to borrow money, dress as if you have plenty of it.

544. Never pick up anything off the floor of a cab.

545. Ask about a store's return policy when you purchase an item that costs more than $50.

546. Remember that kids might be born with good brains, but they must be taught good manners.

547. Never give your credit card number over the phone if you didn't place the call.

548. Don't judge people by their relatives.

549. Put your address inside your luggage as well as on the outside.

550. Remember that everyone you meet is afraid of something, loves something, and has lost something.

551. Check hotel bills carefully, especially the charges for local and long-distance calls.

552. When someone asks you a question you don't want to answer, smile and respond, "Why do you want to know?"

553. **Talk slow
but think quick.**

The Complete Life's Little Instruction Book

554. Seize every opportunity for additional training in your job.

555. When traveling, leave the good jewelry at home.

556. Don't admire people for their wealth but for the creative and generous ways they put it to use.

557. Never betray a confidence.

558. Never leave the kitchen when something's boiling on the stove.

559. Take along two big safety pins when you travel so that you can pin the drapes shut in your motel room.

560 Say "bless you" when you hear someone sneeze.

561. Never give anybody a fondue set or anything painted avocado green.

562. Remember that just the moment you say, "I give up," someone else seeing the same situation is saying, "My, what a great opportunity."

563. Never claim a victory prematurely.

564. Make the punishment fit the crime.

565. Tour the main branch of the public library on Fifth Avenue the next time you are in New York City. Unforgettable.

566. Don't let your family get so busy that you don't sit down to at least one meal a day together.

567. When you lose, don't lose the lesson.

568. Remember the three Rs: Respect for self; Respect for others; Responsibility for all your actions.

569. Carry your own alarm clock when traveling. Hotel wake-up calls are sometimes unreliable.

570. Keep the porch light on until all the family is in for the night.

571. Take along a small gift for the host or hostess when you're a dinner guest. A book is a good choice.

572. Plant zucchini only if you have lots of friends.

573. Don't overlook life's small joys while searching for the big ones.

574. Keep a well-stocked first-aid kit in your car and at home.

575. Never be photographed with a cocktail glass in your hand.

576. Don't let a little dispute injure a great friendship.

577. Don't marry a woman who picks at her food.

578. Order a seed catalog. Read it on the day of the first snowfall.

579. Pack a compass and the Nature Company's pocket survival tool when hiking in unfamiliar territory.

580. Read a book about beekeeping.

581. Don't be surprised to discover that luck favors those who are prepared.

582. When lost or in distress, signal in "threes"—three shouts, three gunshots, or three horn blasts.

583. When asked to play the piano, do it without complaining or making excuses.

584. Subscribe to *Consumer Reports* magazine.

585. Take off the convention badge as soon as you leave the convention hall.

586. Don't expect your love alone to make a neat person out of a messy one.

587. Read the ten books nominated each year for the BookSense Book of the Year Award.

588. Every so often, invite the person in line behind you to go ahead of you.

589. Carry a small pocket knife.

590. Remember that the person who steals an egg will steal a chicken.

591. Meet occasionally with someone who holds vastly different views than you.

592. Don't go looking for trouble.

593. Don't buy someone else's trouble.

594. Be the first to fight for a just cause.

595. Avoid approaching horses and restaurants from the rear.

596. Never say anything uncomplimentary about another person's dog.

597. Give people more than they expect and do it cheerfully.

598. Remember that no time is ever wasted that makes two people better friends.

599. Remember that no time spent with your children is ever wasted.

600. There are people who will always come up with reasons why you can't do what you want to do. Ignore them.

601. Check to see if your regular car insurance covers you when you rent a car. The insurance offered by car rental companies is expensive.

602. If you need to bring in a business partner, make sure he or she brings along some money.

603. If you have trouble with a company's products or services, go to the top. Write the president, then follow up with a phone call.

604. Don't ride in a car if the driver has been drinking.

605. Think twice before accepting the lowest bid.

606. Steer clear of any place with a "Dishwasher Wanted" sign in the window.

607. Never miss a chance to dance with your wife.

608. When in doubt about what art to put on a wall, choose a framed black-and-white photo by Ansel Adams.

609. When boarding a bus, say "hello" to the driver. Say "thank you" when you get off.

610. When uncertain what to wear, a blue blazer, worn with gray wool slacks, a white shirt, and a red-and-blue striped silk tie, is almost always appropriate.

611. Write a short note inside the front cover when giving a book as a gift.

612. Never give a gift that's not beautifully wrapped.

613. Make the rules for your children clear, fair, and consistent.

614. Don't think expensive sports equipment will make up for lack of talent or practice.

615. Learn to say "I love you" in French, Italian, and Swedish.

616. On a clear night, look for Orion's Belt and think of your mother. It's her favorite constellation.

617. Call the Better Business Bureau if you're not sure about a business's reputation.

618. Memorize your favorite love poem.

619. Ask anyone giving you directions to repeat them at least twice.

620. When you are totally exhausted but have to keep going, wash your face and hands and put on clean socks and a clean shirt. You will feel remarkably refreshed.

621. Make allowances for your friends' imperfections as readily as you do for your own.

The Complete Life's Little Instruction Book

622. Be ruthlessly realistic when it comes to your finances.

623. Smile when picking up the phone. The caller will hear it in your voice.

624. Set high goals for your employees and help them attain them.

625. Pay your bills on time. If you can't, write your creditors a letter describing your situation. Send them something every month, even if it's only five dollars.

626. When you realize you've made a mistake, take immediate steps to correct it.

627. Do your homework and know your facts, but remember it's passion that persuades.

628. Don't waste time trying to appreciate music you dislike. Spend time with music you love.

629. Do the right thing, regardless of what others think.

630. Always put something in the collection plate.

631. When concluding a business deal and the other person suggests working out the details later, say, "I understand, but I would like to settle the entire matter right now." Don't move from the table until you do.

632. Ask yourself if you would feel comfortable giving your best friend a key to your house. If not, look for a new best friend.

633. Judge people from where they stand, not from where you stand.

634. Wear a coat and tie to job interviews, even for a job unloading boxcars.

635. Buy a used car with the same caution a naked man uses to climb a barbed-wire fence.

636. Life will sometimes hand you a magical moment. Savor it.

637. Set aside your dreams for your children and help them attain their own dreams.

638. Never wash a car, mow a yard, or select a Christmas tree after dark.

639. Learn how to make tapioca pudding and peanut brittle in the microwave.

640. Dress a little better than your clients but not as well as your boss.

641. Take the stairs when it's four flights or less.

642. Never threaten if you don't intend to back it up.

643. When shaking a woman's hand, squeeze it no harder than she squeezes yours.

644. Be open and accessible. The next person you meet could become your best friend.

645. Hold yourself to the highest standards.

646. Buy the big bottle of Tabasco.

647. Be the first to forgive.

648. Don't confuse comfort with happiness.

649. Don't confuse wealth with success.

650. When talking to your doctor, don't let him or her interrupt or end the session early. It's your body and your money. Stay until all your questions are answered to your satisfaction.

651. Check for toilet paper before sitting down.

652. Whenever you take something back for an exchange or refund, wear a coat and tie.

653. Don't stop the parade to pick up a dime.

654. Make a habit of reading something inspiring and cheerful just before going to sleep.

655. Remember that a person who is foolish with money is foolish in other ways too.

656. Marry a woman you love to talk to. As you get older, her conversational skills will be as important as any other.

657. If you work for an organization that makes its decisions by committee, make darn sure you're on the committee.

658. When hiring, give special consideration to a man who is an Eagle Scout and a woman who has received the Girl Scout Gold Award.

659. Turn enemies into friends by doing something nice for them.

660. Be as friendly to the janitor as you are to the chairman of the board.

661. Never buy anything electical at a flea market.

662. If you want to do something and you feel in your bones that it's the right thing to do, do it. Intuition is often as important as the facts.

663. Don't cut corners.

664. Learn to bake bread.

665. Everyone loves praise. Look for ways to give it to them.

666. Stand when shaking someone's hand.

667. Be an original. If that means being a little eccentric, so be it.

668. Everybody deserves a birthday cake. Never celebrate a birthday without one.

669. Open your arms to change, but don't let go of your values.

670. When it comes to worrying or painting a picture, know when to stop.

671. Don't expect anyone to know what you want for Christmas if you don't tell them.

672. Before taking a long trip, fill your tank and empty your bladder.

673. Ask for double prints when you have film processed. Send the extras to the people in the photos.

674. Be quick to take advantage of an advantage.

675. Pay as much attention to the things that are working positively in your life as you do to those that are giving you trouble.

676. Mind your own business.

677. When taking a woman home, make sure she's safely inside her house before you leave.

678. Live with your new pet several days before you name it. The right name will come to you.

679. Every year celebrate the day you and your wife had your first date.

680. Treat your employees with the same respect you give your clients.

681. Slow down. I mean really slow down in school zones.

682. Allow your children to face the consequences of their actions.

683. Don't expect the best gifts to come wrapped in the prettiest paper.

684. You may be fortunate and make a lot of money, but be sure your work involves something that enriches your spirit as well as your bank account.

685. When a good man or woman runs for political office, support him or her with your time and money.

686. When you need professional advice, get it from professionals, not from your friends.

687. Don't buy a cheap mattress.

688. Remember that silence is sometimes the best answer.

689. Don't think you can relax your way to happiness. Happiness comes as a result of doing.

690. Don't dismiss a good idea simply because you don't like the source.

691. Pay for a disadvantaged child to go to summer camp.

692. What you must do, do cheerfully.

693. Don't believe all you hear, spend all you have, or sleep all you want.

694. Choose a church that sings joyful music.

695. Don't waste time waiting for inspiration. Begin, and inspiration will find you.

696. When you say, "I love you," mean it.

697. When you say, "I'm sorry," look the person in the eye.

698. Be engaged at least six months before you get married.

699. Conduct yourself in such a way that your high school would want you to address the graduating seniors.

700. Win without boasting.

701. Lose without excuses.

702. Choose the apartment on the top floor.

703. Ask someone you'd like to know better to list five people he or she would most like to meet. It will tell you a lot about that person.

704. Watch your attitude. It's the first thing people notice about you.

705. Don't be a person who says, "Ready, fire, aim."

706. Don't be a person who says, "Ready, aim, aim, aim."

707. Deadlines are important. Meet them.

708. When you find someone doing small things well, put him or her in charge of bigger things.

709. Pack a light bathrobe on overnight trips. Take your pillow, too.

710. Read more books.

711. Watch less TV.

712. Remember that a good price is not necessarily what an object is marked, but what it is worth to you.

713. Buy three best-selling children's books. Read them and then give them to a youngster.

714. When opportunity knocks, invite it to stay for dinner.

715. Remember that the more you know, the less you fear.

716. When a waitress or waiter provides exceptional service, leave a generous tip, plus a short note such as, "Thanks for the wonderful service. You made our meal a special experience."

717. Remove your sunglasses when you talk to someone.

718. Become your children's best teacher and coach.

719. Introduce yourself to your neighbors as soon as you move into a new neighborhood.

720. When a friend or loved one becomes ill, remember that hope and positive thinking are strong medicines.

721. When you find something you really want, don't let a few dollars keep you from getting it.

722. Don't confuse mere inconveniences with real problems.

723. Some things need doing better than they've ever been done before. Some just need doing. Others don't need doing at all. Know which is which.

724. Buy ladders, extension cords, and garden hoses longer than you think you'll need.

725. When asked to pray in public, be quick about it.

726. Show extra respect for people whose jobs put dirt under their fingernails.

727. Hold your child's hand every chance you get. The time will come all too soon when he or she won't let you.

728. When you carve the Thanksgiving turkey, give the first piece to the person who prepared it.

729. Live a good, honorable life. Then when you get older and think back, you'll get to enjoy it a second time.

730. Learn to juggle.

731. Remember that a good example is the best sermon.

732. Wipe off the sticky honey jar before putting it back on the shelf.

733. Purchase one piece of original art each year, even if it's just a small painting by a high school student.

734. Volunteer to work a few hours each month in a soup kitchen.

735. If you're treated unfairly by an airline, contact the Consumer Affairs Office of the Department of Transportation at (202) 366-2220.

736. Don't think people at the top of their professions have all the answers. They don't.

737. Remember the wisdom of the old proverb, "Out of debt, out of danger."

738. Get a car with a sun roof.

739. When traveling by plane, don't pack valuables or important papers in your suitcase. Carry them on board with you.

740. Don't carry expensive luggage. It's a tip-off to thieves that expensive items may be inside.

741. Keep your private thoughts private.

742. Once every couple of months enjoy a four-course meal—but eat each course at a different restaurant.

743. Introduce yourself to someone you would like to meet by smiling, giving your name, and saying, "I haven't had the pleasure of meeting you."

744. Put your jacket around your girlfriend on a chilly evening.

745. Be humble and polite, but don't let anyone push you around.

746. Put the strap around your neck before looking through binoculars.

747. Do 100 push-ups every day: 50 in the morning and 50 in the evening.

748. Wear safety glasses when operating a Weed Eater or power saw.

749. Wrap a couple of thick rubber bands around your wallet when you're fishing or hiking. This will prevent it from slipping out of your pocket.

750. Don't expect bankers to come to your aid in a financial crunch.

751. Be advised that when negotiating, if you don't get it in writing, you probably won't get it.

752. Don't do business with anyone who has a history of suing people.

753. Trust in God, but lock your car.

The Complete Life's Little Instruction Book

754. Every so often let your spirit of adventure triumph over your good sense.

755. Use a favorite picture of a loved one as a bookmark.

756. Never lose your nerve, your temper, or your car keys.

757. Add to your children's private library by giving them a hardback copy of one of the classics every birthday. Begin with their first birthday.

758. Surprise an old friend with a phone call.

759. Champion your wife. Be her best friend and biggest fan.

760. Carry a list of your wife's important sizes in your wallet.

761. Don't open credit card bills on the weekend. Wait until Monday.

762. Mind the store. No one cares about your business the way you do.

763. Don't say no until you've heard the whole story.

764. When you are a dinner guest, take a second helping if it's offered, but never a third.

765. Never say anything uncomplimentary about your wife or children in the presence of others.

766. Before going to bed on Christmas Eve, join hands with your family and sing "Silent Night."

767. Get involved at your child's school.

768. Don't accept unacceptable behavior.

769. Judge your job not by what you're making, but what it's making of you.

770. When eating at a restaurant that features foreign food, don't order anything you can fix at home.

771. When giving a speech, concentrate on what you can give the audience, not what you can get from them.

The Complete Life's Little Instruction Book

772. Send your mother-in-law flowers on your wife's birthday.

773. Write your pastor a note and tell him how much he means to you.

774. Apologize immediately when you lose your temper, especially to children.

775. When you're uncertain of what you should pay someone, ask, "What do you think is fair?" You'll almost always get a reasonable answer.

776. Write your favorite author a note of appreciation

777. When you know that someone has gone to a lot of trouble to get dressed up, tell them they look terrific!

778. A loving atmosphere in your home is so important. Do all you can to create a tranquil, harmonious environment.

779. When you tell a child to do something, don't follow it with, "Okay?" Ask instead, "Do you understand?"

780. Don't let weeds
grow around
your dreams.

781. Remember that almost everything looks better after a good night's sleep.

782. Buy your fiancé the nicest diamond engagement ring you can afford.

783. Don't be so concerned with your rights that you forget your manners.

784. Stop and watch stonemasons at work.

785. Stop and watch a farmer plowing a field.

786. Avoid using the word *impacted* unless you are describing wisdom teeth.

787. Read William Safire's *Lend Me Your Ears,* a collection of the world's great speeches (W. W. Norton & Co., 2004).

788. Keep a separate shaving kit packed just for traveling.

789. Remember that *how* you say something is as important as *what* you say.

790. Every so often watch *Sesame Street.*

791. When you see visitors taking pictures of each other, offer to take a picture of them together.

792. In disagreements with loved ones, deal with the current situation. Don't bring up the past.

793. Never apologize for extreme measures when defending your values, your health, or your family's safety.

794. Get to garage sales early. The good stuff is usually gone by 8:00 a.m.

795. If your town has a baseball team, attend the season opener.

796. Don't think you can fill an emptiness in your heart with money.

797. Become famous for finishing important, difficult tasks.

798. Leave a quarter where a child can find it.

799. Read between the lines.

800. Never sell your teddy bear, letter sweater, or high school yearbooks at a garage sale. You'll regret it later.

801. Make a video of the contents of your home for insurance purposes. Don't forget closets and drawers. Burn a DVD of the footage and store it in your bank safe-deposit box.

802. When you're lost, admit it, and ask for directions.

803. Don't take good friends, good health, or a good marriage for granted.

804. Don't gamble. Remember that billion-dollar casinos were built on their winnings, not yours.

805. Buy a new tie to wear at your wedding rehearsal dinner. Wear it only once. Keep it forever.

806. Never buy just one roll of toilet paper, one roll of film, or one jar of peanut butter. Get two.

807. Never type a love letter. Use a fountain pen.

808. Do a good job because you want to, not because you have to. This puts you in charge instead of your boss.

809. Remember that the shortest way to get anywhere is to have good company traveling with you.

810. Never buy a chair or sofa without first sitting on it for several minutes.

811. Never eat liver at a restaurant. Some things should be done only in the privacy of one's home.

812. Don't be thin-skinned. Take criticism as well as praise with equal grace.

813. At the end of your days, be leaning forward—not falling backwards.

814. Keep impeccable tax records.

815. Clean out a different drawer in your house every week.

816. When working with contractors, include a penalty clause in your contract for their not finishing on time.

817. Read bulletin boards at the grocery store, college bookstore, and coin laundry. You will find all sorts of interesting things there.

818. The next time you're standing next to a police officer, firefighter, or paramedic, tell them that you appreciate what they do for the community.

819. Learn three knock-knock jokes so that you will always be ready to entertain children.

820. Share your knowledge. It's a way to achieve immortality.

821. Don't work for a company led by someone of questionable character.

822. Visit your old high school and introduce yourself to the principal. Ask if you can sit in on a couple of classes.

823. In a verbal confrontation, lower your voice to the degree that the other person raises his or hers.

824. Be gentle with
the earth.

825. Spend your time and energy creating, not criticizing.

826. Show respect when riding sailboats, snowmobiles, and motorcycles. They can teach you a painful lesson very fast.

827. Act with courtesy and fairness regardless of how others treat you. Don't let them determine your response.

828. Don't leave hair in the shower drain.

The Complete Life's Little Instruction Book

829. Let your children see you do things for your wife that lets them know how much you love and treasure her.

830. Take photographs of every car you own. Later, these photos will trigger wonderful memories.

831. Don't allow children to ride in the back of a pickup truck.

832. When you are a dinner guest at a restaurant, don't order anything more expensive than your host does.

833. When someone offers to pay you now or later, choose now.

834. When traveling the backroads, stop whenever you see a sign that reads "Honey For Sale."

835. Start every day with the most important thing you have to do. Save the less important tasks for later.

836. Refuse to share personal and financial information unless you feel it is absolutely essential.

837. Don't outlive your money.

838. Never grab at a falling knife.

839. When there is a hill to climb, don't think that waiting will make it smaller.

840. Don't call a fishing rod a "pole," a line a "rope," a rifle a "gun," or a ship a "boat."

841. When your dog dies, frame his collar and put it above a window facing west.

842. When a garment label warns "Dry Clean Only," believe it.

843. Never take what you cannot use.

844. Just because you earn a decent wage, don't look down on those who don't. To put things in perspective, consider what would happen to the public good if you didn't do your job for 30 days. Then, consider the consequences if sanitation workers didn't do their jobs for 30 days. Now, whose job is more important?

845. Don't eat any meat loaf but your mom's.

846. Write the date and the names of non-family members on the backs of all photos as soon as you get them from the developer.

847. Don't take 11 items to the 10 Items Express Check-Out lane.

848. Think twice before deciding not to charge for your work. People often don't value what they don't pay for.

849. Pray. There is immeasurable power in it.

The Complete Life's Little Instruction Book

850. Help a child plant a small garden.

851. At meetings, resist turning around to see who has just arrived late.

852. Don't ride a bicycle or motorcycle barefooted.

853. Don't purchase anything in a package that appears to have been opened.

854. Overestimate travel time by fifteen percent.

855. Never do business with people who knock on your door and say, "I just happened to be in the neighborhood."

856. Never eat a sugared doughnut when wearing a dark suit.

857. Call a nursing home or retirement center and ask for a list of the residents who seldom get mail or visitors. Send them a card several times a year. Sign it, "Someone who thinks you are very special."

858. Choose a business partner the way you choose a tennis partner. Select someone who's strong where you are weak.

859. Make duplicates of all important keys.

860. Read a lot when you're on vacation, but nothing that has to do with your business.

861. Put the knife in the jelly before putting it in the peanut butter when you make a PB&J sandwich.

862. Remember that what's right isn't always popular, and what's popular isn't always right.

863. Before buying a house or renting an apartment, check the water pressure by turning on the faucets and the shower and then flushing the toilet.

864. Properly fitting shoes should feel good as soon as you try them on. Don't believe the salesperson who says, "They'll be fine as soon as you break them in."

865. Schedule your bachelor party at least two days before your wedding.

866. Get a haircut at least a week before the big interview.

867. Spend your life lifting people up, not putting people down.

868. Never interrupt when you're being flattered.

869. Don't pick up after your children. That's their job.

870. Remember that
great love and
great achievements
involve great risk.

871. Own a cowboy hat.

872. Own a comfortable chair
for reading.

873. Own a set of good kitchen knives.

874. In business or in life, don't follow the
wagon tracks too closely.

875. Never order chicken-fried steak at a
place where you don't see a couple
of pickup trucks in the parking lot.

876. Get your name off mailing lists by writing to: Mail Preference Service, P.O. Box 643, Carmel, NY 10512 or go to www.dmaconsumers.org/offmailinglist.html.

877. Brush your teeth before putting on your tie.

878. Never risk what you can't afford to lose.

879. Don't trust a woman who doesn't close her eyes when you kiss her.

880. Never tell a man he's losing his hair. He already knows.

881. Learn to use a needle and thread, a steam iron, and an espresso machine.

882. Remember that the "suggested retail price" seldom is.

883. Never say, "My child would never do that."

884. Once a year, go someplace you've never been before.

885. Replace the batteries in smoke alarms every January 1st.

886. Remember that ignorance is expensive.

887. Keep candles and matches in the kitchen and bedroom in case of power failure.

888. If you make a lot of money, put it to use helping others while you are living. That is wealth's greatest satisfaction.

889. Listen to your critics. But keep your own counsel.

890. Learn to make great spaghetti sauce.

891. Never say anything to a news reporter that you don't want to see on the front page of your local paper. Comments made "off the record" seldom are.

892. Don't allow your dog to bark and disturb the neighbors.

893. Remember that not getting what you want is sometimes a stroke of good luck.

894. Never tell a person who's experiencing deep sorrow, "I know how you feel." You don't.

895. When declaring your rights, don't forget your responsibilities.

896. Remember that what you give will afford you more pleasure than what you get.

897. Display your street number
prominently on your mailbox or
house in case emergency vehicles
need to find you.

898. Think twice before accepting a job
that requires you to work in an office
with no windows.

899. Never hire someone you wouldn't
invite home to dinner.

900. When camping or hiking, never
leave evidence that you were there.

901. Remember that everyone you meet wears an invisible sign. It reads, "Notice me. Make me feel important."

902. Perform your job better than anyone else can. That's the best job security I know.

903. Dress respectfully when attending church.

904. Whether it's life or a horse that throws you, get right back on.

905. When you have the choice of two exciting things, choose the one you haven't tried.

906. Learn to save on even the most modest salary. If you do, you're almost assured of financial success.

907. Never ask an accountant, lawyer, or doctor professional questions in a social setting.

908. For easier reading in motel rooms, pack your own 100-watt light bulb.

909. When someone has provided you with exceptional service, write a note to his or her boss.

910. Look your best the day you ask for a raise, request a loan, or appear in court.

911. When lending people money, be sure their character exceeds their collateral.

912. Hang up if someone puts you on hold to take a "call waiting."

913. Be cautious telling people how contented and happy you are. Some will resent it.

914. Accept the fact that regardless of how many times you are right, you will sometimes be wrong.

915. No matter how old you get, hug and kiss your mother whenever you greet her.

916. Watch *The Andy Griffith Show* to help keep things in perspective.

917. Learn the rules.
Then break some.

The Complete Life's Little Instruction Book

918. Every once in a while ask yourself the question, If money weren't a consideration, what would I like to be doing?

919. Go to local craft fairs.

920. Go to a high school performance of a Broadway musical.

921. Go to chili cook-offs.

922. Put love notes in your child's lunch box.

923. Encourage anyone who is trying to improve mentally, physically, or spiritually.

924. Remember that half the joy of achievement is in the anticipation.

925. Order an L. L. Bean catalog. Write to L. L. Bean, Freeport, ME 04033, or go to www.llbean.com.

926. Order a Sundance catalog. Call 1-800-422-2770 or go to www.sundancecatalog.com.

The Complete Life's Little Instruction Book

927. Remember that the best relationship is one where your love for each other is greater than your need for each other.

928. When you need assistance, ask this way: "I've got a problem. I wonder if you would be kind enough to help me?"

929. Get involved with your local government. As someone said, "Politics is too important to be left to the politicians."

930. Never swap your integrity for money, power, or fame.

931. Call your local police department and ask about riding with an officer on night patrol.

932. Never sell yourself short.

933. Put on old clothes before you get out the paint brushes.

934. Learn to play "Amazing Grace" on the piano.

935. Fool someone on April 1st.

936. Never remind someone of a kindness or act of generosity you have shown him or her. Bestow a favor and then forget it.

937. Help your children set up their own savings and checking accounts by age 16.

938. Visit friends and relatives when they are in the hospital. You only need to stay a few minutes.

939. Never be ashamed of your patriotism.

940. Never be ashamed of honest tears.

941. Never be ashamed of laughter that's too loud or singing that's too joyful.

942. Always try the house dressing.

943. Do all you can to increase the salaries of good teachers.

944. When you get really angry, stick your hands in your pockets.

945. Don't trust your memory; write it down.

946. At least once, date a woman with beautiful red hair.

947. Watch the movie *Regarding Henry*.

948. Watch the movie *Mr. Smith Goes to Washington*.

949. Attach a small Christmas wreath to your car's grill on the first day of December.

950. Judge your success
by what you had to
give up in order
to get it.

951. Never leave a youngster in the car without taking the car keys.

952. Don't think that sending a gift or flowers substitutes for your presence.

953. When visiting a small town at lunch time, choose the café on the square.

954. Never ask a barber if you need a haircut.

955. Never "borrow" so much as a pencil from your workplace.

956. Truth is serious business. When criticizing others, remember that a little goes a long way.

957. Never buy a piece of jewelry that costs more than $100 without doing a little haggling.

958. When your children are learning to play musical instruments, buy them good ones.

959. Be especially courteous and patient with older people.

960. Become a tourist for a day in your own hometown. Take a tour. See the sights.

961. Don't confuse foolishness with bravery.

962. Don't mistake kindness for weakness.

963. Don't discuss domestic problems at work.

964. Answer the easy questions first.

965. Never ignore evil.

The Complete Life's Little Instruction Book

966. A racehorse that consistently runs just a second faster than another horse is worth millions of dollars more. Be willing to give that extra effort that separates the winner from the one in second place.

967. Create a smoke-free office and home.

968. Never get a tattoo.

969. Remember that no two people looking out the same window see exactly the same thing.

970. Let some things remain mysterious.

971. When you are away from home and hear church bells, think of someone who loves you.

972. Remember this statement by Coach Lou Holtz: "Life is 10 percent what happens to me and 90 percent how I react to it."

973. Travel. See new places, but remember to take along an open mind.

974. Buy a small, inexpensive camera.
Take it with you everywhere.

975. When friends offer to help, let them.

976. Never decide to do nothing just
because you can only do a little.
Do what you can.

977. Acknowledge every gift, no matter
how small.

978. Every now and then, bite off more
than you can chew.

979. Remember that your character is your destiny.

980. Approach love and cooking with reckless abandon.

981. Grind it out. Hanging on just one second longer than your competition makes you the winner.

982. Buy and use your customers' products.

983. Be better prepared than you think you need to be.

984. Call before dropping in on friends and family.

985. Let your handshake be as binding as a signed contract.

986. Keep and file the best business letters you receive.

987. Pay the extra money for the best seats at a play or concert.

988. Give handout materials after your presentation, never before.

989. Never buy anything from a rude salesperson, no matter how much you want it.

990. Get a flu shot.

991. Worry makes for a hard pillow. When something's troubling you, before going to sleep, jot down three things you can do the next day to help solve the problem.

992. Hire people more for their judgment than for their talents.

993. Life is short. Eat more pancakes and fewer rice cakes.

994. Buy a red umbrella. It's easier to find among all the black ones, and it adds a little color to rainy days.

995. Love someone who doesn't deserve it.

996. Every so often, go where you can hear a wooden screen door slam shut.

996. When you mean no, say it in a way that's not ambiguous.

998. Never open a restaurant.

999. Attend a high school football game. Sit near the band.

1000. Give children toys that are powered by their imagination, not by batteries.

1001. Remember that your child's character is like good soup. Both are homemade.

1002. When you're buying something that you only need to buy once, buy the best you can afford.

1003. As soon as you get married, start saving for your children's education.

1004. Reject and condemn prejudice based on race, gender, religion, or age.

1005. Be suspicious of a boss who schedules meetings instead of making decisions.

1006. Choose a seat in the row next to the emergency exit when flying. You will get more leg room.

1007. Get involved with Habitat for Humanity and help build housing for the poor. Call 1-800-HABITAT, or go to www.habitat.org.

1008. You may dress unconventionally, but remember, the more strangely you dress, the better you have to be.

1009. Carry three business cards in your wallet.

1010. Regardless of the situation, react with class.

1011. For emergencies, always have two quarters in your pocket and a ten-dollar bill hidden in your wallet.

1012. Don't overfeed horses or brothers-in-law.

1013. Be able to hit consistently three out of five baskets at the free-throw line.

1014. Remember the observation of William James that the deepest principle in human nature is the craving to be appreciated.

1015. Become the kind of person who brightens a room just by entering it.

1016. Buy raffle tickets, candy bars, and baked goods from students who are raising money for school projects.

1017. Be wary of the man who's "all hat and no cattle."

1018. Borrow a box of puppies for an afternoon and take them to visit the residents of a retirement home. Stand back and watch the smiles.

1019. Never forget that it takes only one person or one idea to change your life forever.

The Complete Life's Little Instruction Book

1020. Reread Thoreau's *Walden.*

1021. When there's a piano to be moved, don't reach for the stool.

1022. Go on blind dates. Remember, that's how I met your mother.

1023. Root for the home team.

1024. Follow your own star.

1025. Remember the ones who love you.

1026. Go home for the holidays.

1027. Don't get too big for your britches.

1028. Call your dad.

Volume III

1029. Never buy a coffee table you can't put your feet on.

1030. Say something positive as early as possible every day.

1031. Believe in miracles but don't depend on them.

1032. Never open the refrigerator when you're bored.

1033. Fill out expense reports the day you return from your trip.

1034. Regardless of the situation, remember that nothing is ever lost by courtesy.

1035. Own at least one article of clothing with Mickey Mouse on it.

1036. When staying at a hotel or motel, don't accept a room next to the ice or vending machines.

1037. Never go near a kid who's holding a water hose unless you want to get wet.

1038. Be thankful you were born in this great country.

1039. Enjoy the satisfaction that comes from doing little things well.

1040. Never refuse a holiday dessert.

1041. If you are involved in an automobile accident, don't admit fault (there may be extenuating circumstances) and don't discuss the accident with anyone except the police and your insurance agent.

1042. Encourage your children to join a choir.

1043. Never allow anyone to intimidate you.

1044. Watch your finances like a hawk.

1045. Don't forget that we are ultimately judged by what we give, not by what we get.

1046. Read Tom Peters' *The Pursuit of WOW!* (Vintage, 1994).

1047. Always compliment flower gardens and new babies.

1048. When you're a passenger in someone else's car, never complain about the music.

1049. Remember that it's better to be cheated in price than in quality.

1050. Pack a couple of Ziploc bags and a pad of Post-it notes when you travel.

1051. Don't allow your children or grandchildren to call you by your first name.

1052. When reading self-help books,
include the Bible.

1053. Each year, take a first-day-of-school
photograph of your children.

1054. Learn the rules of the sports your
children play.

1055. When you hear a kind word spoken
about a friend, tell him so.

1056. Never hesitate to do what you
know is right.

1057. Don't work for recognition, but do work worthy of recognition.

1058. Be charitable in your speech, actions, and judgment.

1059. Work for a company where the expectations of you are high.

1060. Remember that a kind word goes a long way.

1061. Don't compare your children with their siblings or classmates.

1062. Be enthusiastic in your expressions of gratitude and appreciation.

1063. Ask permission before taking someone's photograph.

1064. Join the Rotary or another civic club.

1065. When no great harm will result, let your children do it their way, even if you know they are wrong. They will learn more from their mistakes than from their successes.

1066. Type out your favorite quotation and place it where you can see it every day.

1067. Forgive quickly.

1068. Kiss slowly.

1069. Tell your wife often how terrific she looks.

1070. Remember that regardless of where you are, not much good happens after midnight.

1071. Never give an anniversary gift that has to be plugged in.

1072. Remember that the word *discipline* means "to teach."

1073. Remember that all success comes at a price.

1074. When you give someone a camera as a gift, be sure it's loaded with film and has a battery.

1075. Tour your state capitol building.

1076. Earn your success based on service to others, not at the expense of others.

1077. Never say anything uncomplimentary about your wife in the presence of your children.

1078. Remember the three universal healers: calamine lotion, warm oatmeal, and hugs.

1079. To fight the blues, try exercising.

1080. Never watch a movie or video with your children that involves activities and language you don't want them to imitate.

1081. Share your knowledge and experiences.

1082. Volunteer to be a Little League umpire.

1083. If you wear a tuxedo twice a year or more, buy your own.

1084. Kiss your children good night, even if they are already asleep.

1085. Compliment the parent when you observe a well-behaved child.

1086. Learn the Heimlich maneuver.

1087. When traveling, sleep with your
wallet, car keys, room key,
eyeglasses, and shoes nearby.

1088. Never pass up a chance to be in a
parade.

1089. Start the standing ovation at the
end of school plays.

1090. Remember the credo of Walt Disney:
Think. Believe. Dream. Dare.

1091. Spend twice as much time praising as you do criticizing.

1092. When someone lets you down, don't give up on them.

1093. Treat your company's money as you would your own.

1094. Remember that life's big changes rarely give advance warning.

1095. What you have to do, do wholeheartedly.

1096. Teach your children never to underestimate someone with a disability.

1097. Never comment on someone's weight unless you know it's what they want to hear.

1098. Find a job you love and give it everything you've got.

1099. Make a list of travel necessities, laminate it, and keep it in your suitcase.

1100. Read the *Wall Street Journal* regularly.

1101. Keep good financial records.

1102. Never complain about a flight delayed for mechanical repairs. Waiting on the ground is infinitely better than the alternative.

1103. Don't hand out your troubles to your friends and co-workers.

1104. Occasionally let your children help you, even if it slows you down.

1105. Set limits on the amount and content of television your children watch.

1106. Seek respect rather than popularity.

1107. Seek quality rather than luxury.

1108. Seek refinement rather than fashion.

1109. Take your teenagers with you when you buy a car or expensive household item and let them learn from the experience.

1110. Throw a surprise birthday party for a friend.

1111. Always take your vacation time.

1112. Take some silly photos of yourself and a friend in an instant photo booth.

1113. Start a "smile file" of jokes, articles, and cartoons that make you laugh.

1114. Start a "read again file" for articles you might want to enjoy a second time.

1115. Someone will always be looking at you as an example of how to behave. Don't let that person down.

1116. When you need a little advice, call your grandparents.

1117. Teach your sons as well as your daughters to cook.

1118. Look for the opportunity that's hidden in every adversity.

1119. Don't sit while ladies are standing.

1120. Remember that when your mom says, "You'll regret it," you probably will.

1121. Report unethical business practices to your city's Better Business Bureau.

1122. Don't be critical of your wife's friends.

1123. Be prompt when picking up or dropping off your children for school or other activities.

1124. Once a month invite someone to lunch who knows more about your business than you.

1125. Become a serious student of American history.

1126. Make a big batch of Rice Krispies squares. Take them to the office.

1127. Play catch with a kid.

1128. Write some poetry.

1129. Shoot a few hoops.

1130. To open a bottle of champagne, hold the cork and twist the bottle.

1131. Never ignore an old barking dog.

1132. To put someone in your debt, do something nice for their child.

1133. Improve even the best sausage biscuit by spreading on a little grape jelly.

1134. Try to add a new name to your Rolodex every week.

1135. Never criticize your country when traveling abroad.

1136. If you are not going to use a discount coupon, leave it on the shelf with the product for someone else to use.

1137. When loved ones drive away, watch and wave until you can no longer see the car.

1138. On your birthday, send your mom a thank-you card.

1139. Never tell an off-color joke in the presence of women or children.

1140. Respect your elders.

1141. Keep a pad and pencil by every phone.

1142. If you dial a wrong number, don't just hang up; offer an apology.

1143. Hold yourself to the same high standards that you require of others.

1144. Get someone's attention by saying, "I just heard the nicest compliment about you."

1145. Never let the odds keep you from pursuing what you know in your heart you were meant to do.

1146. Spend a couple of hours each week reading magazines that have nothing to do with your job or lifestyle.

1147. Wage war against procrastination.

1148. Don't open anyone else's mail.

1149. Never loan your chain saw, your ball glove, or your favorite book.

1150. Keep a roll of duct tape at home, at the office, and in your car.

1151. Learn the techniques of being a good interviewer.

1152. Add Garrison Keillor's collection of poems entitled *Good Poems* (Viking, 2002) to your home library.

1153. When the "best in the world" visits your town for a concert, exhibition, or speech, get tickets to attend.

1154. Remember that a lasting marriage is built on commitment, not convenience.

1155. Until your children move out of your house, don't buy anything suede.

1156. Buy each of your children a special Christmas ornament every year. When they move into their own homes, box up the ornaments and give them as house-warming gifts.

1157. Offer hope.

1158. Let your word be your bond.

1159. Count your change.

1160. Enter something in the state fair.

1161. When you need to apologize to someone, do it in person.

1162. Try to find a copy of the book *Under My Elm* by David Grayson (Doubleday, 1942). You might have to order it.

1163. Take your child on a tour of a local university.

1164. Finish projects before they are due.

1165. Be happy with what you have while working for what you want.

1166. Never ask a childless couple when they are going to have children.

1167. Let your children observe your being generous to those in need.

1168. Celebrate even small victories.

1169. Never answer a reporter's questions with, "No comment." Instead, say, "I don't have enough information to comment on that right now."

1170. Cut your fingernails in private.

1171. After going to bed, refuse to worry about problems until the morning.

1172. Return shopping carts to the designated areas.

1173. Attend an Eagle Scout's or a Girl Scout's Golden Award induction ceremony.

1174. Never tell a car salesman how much you want to spend.

1175. Redeem gift certificates promptly.

1176. Remember that a grateful heart is almost always a happy one.

1177. Make every effort to attend weddings and funerals of family and friends.

1178. Don't forget that a couple of words of praise or encouragement can make someone's day.

1179. Be especially courteous to receptionists and secretaries; they are the gatekeepers.

1180. Every year, send your old alma mater a few bucks.

1181. Make your money before spending it.

1182. Don't overschedule your children's extracurricular activities.

1183. Whenever you hear an ambulance siren, say a prayer for the person inside.

1184. Don't take medicine in the dark.

1185. Spoil your wife,
not your children.

The Complete Life's Little Instruction Book

1186. Worry about the consequences of the choices you make before you make them—not afterward.

1187. Attend parent-teacher conferences and PTA meetings.

1188. Stop and look up when anyone approaches your desk.

1189. Get a passport and keep it current.

1190. Remember that no one ever became famous for turning back.

1191. Search out good values, but let the
other guy make a fair profit on what
you purchase.

1192. Be cautious of renting lodging
accommodations described in
the ad or brochure as "rustic."

1193. Insist that your children complete
a driver's education course at
their school.

1194. Get to know your children's
teachers.

1195. Locate the emergency exits on your floor as soon as you check into your hotel room.

1196. Stay humble.

1197. Stay on your toes.

1198. Write a letter to the editor at least once a year.

1199. When playing a sport with a partner, never criticize his or her performance.

1200. Remember that you can miss a lot of good things in life by having the wrong attitude.

The Complete Life's Little Instruction Book

1201. Support your local museums.

1202. Support your local symphony.

1203. Support your community college.

1204. If you are a guest at a wedding,
       take lots of snapshots and send
       them to the bride and groom as
       quickly as you can. They have a
       long time to wait for the formal
       pictures and will be thrilled to
       receive the ones you took.

1205. Know where to find a gas station that's open twenty-four hours with a working bathroom.

1206. Hang up on anyone you don't know who's trying to sell you a financial product over the telephone.

1207. When a guest, never complain about the food, drink, or accommodations.

1208. Require your children to do their share of household chores.

1209. Take a course in public speaking.

1210. For better security when traveling, take along a small wedge of wood and jam it under your hotel room door.

1211. Own a salad spinner.

1212. Underestimate when guessing an adult's age or weight.

1213. Overestimate when guessing someone's salary.

1214. Never leave a loved one in anger.

1215. Choose a clothing salesperson who dresses as you wish you did.

1216. Send notes of encouragement to military personnel and college students.

1217. Occasionally leave a quarter in the change return slot of a pay phone. Somebody always checks.

1218. When in doubt, smile.

1219. Overpay the neighborhood kid who does yard work for you.

1220. When a friend is in need, help him without his having to ask.

1221. Keep an empty gas can in your trunk.

1222. Own two crystal champagne glasses.

1223 Allow drivers from out of state a little extra room on the road.

1224. Never criticize a gift.

1225. Volunteer to help at your city's Special Olympics.

1226. Teach your children the pride, satisfaction, and dignity of doing any job well.

1227. Never ask a woman when the baby is due unless you know for sure that she's pregnant.

1228. Never whittle toward yourself.

1229. Make a generous contribution to diabetes research.

1230. Frame anything your child brings home on his first day of school.

1231. Keep $10 in your glove box for emergencies.

1232. When serving hamburgers, always toast the buns.

1233. Marry someone your equal or a little bit better.

1234. Never be
too busy to meet
someone new.

1235. Out of respect and appreciation for the efforts of the cook, don't dress casually for Thanksgiving dinner.

1236. Remember that cruel words deeply hurt.

1237. Remember that loving words quickly heal.

1238. Keep a special notebook. Every night before going to bed, make a note of something beautiful that you saw during the day.

1239. If it's not a beautiful morning, let your cheerfulness make it one.

1240. Plant a tree the day your child is born.

1241. Surprise someone who's more than eighty years old or a couple celebrating fifty years or more of marriage with a personal greeting from the President. Mail details to The White House, Attn: Greetings Office, Washington, DC 20502-0039 or go to www.whitehouse.gov/greeting, four to six weeks in advance.

1242. Don't say anything on a cordless or cellular telephone that you don't want the world to hear.

1243. Never get yourself into a position where you have to back up a trailer.

1244. Toss in a coin when passing a wishing well.

1245. Give young children the opportunity to participate in family decision-making. Their insight will surprise you.

1246. When you're the first one up, be quiet about it.

1247. This year, visit two or three of your state parks.

1248. Remember that a minute of anger denies you sixty seconds of happiness.

1249. Include a recent family photo when writing to a loved one.

1250. Become a Big Brother or Big Sister.

1251. To help your children turn out well, spend twice as much time with them and half as much money.

1252. Ask your grandparents to tell you stories about your parents when they were growing up.

1253. Before criticizing a new employee, remember your first days at work.

1254. Tell family members you love them before they go away for a few days.

1255. Keep a backup copy of your personal address book.

1256. Fill out customer comment cards.

1257. Welcome the unexpected!
Opportunities rarely come in neat,
predictable packages.

1258. Don't make eating everything on
their plate an issue with children.

1259. Never miss an opportunity to go
fishing with your father.

1260. Never miss an opportunity to go
traveling with your mother.

1261. Dust, then vacuum.

1262. Never forget the people who gave you a second chance.

1263. Hold a child's hand when crossing the street.

1264. Do something every day that maintains your good health.

1265. Every spring set out a couple of tomato plants.

1266. When traveling, stop occasionally at local cafés and diners.

1267. Never deny anyone the opportunity to do something nice for you.

1268. Never tell a woman you liked her hair better before she had it cut.

1269. Offer to pay for parking and tolls when you ride with someone.

1270. Offer to leave the tip when someone invites you out to eat.

1271. Remember that a successful future begins right now.

1272. When playing golf and tennis, occasionally play with someone better than you are.

1273. Visit a pet store every once in a while and watch the children watch the animals.

1274. Don't minimize your child's worries and fears.

1275. Take advantage of free lectures on any subject in which you are remotely interested.

1276. Never give up on a dream just because of the length of time it will take to accomplish it. The time will pass anyway.

1277. Unless it creates a safety problem, pull your car over and stop when a funeral procession is passing.

1278. Take your dad bowling.

1279. Be the first adult to jump into the pool or run into the ocean with the kids. They will love you for it.

1280. Hold puppies, kittens, and babies any time you get the chance.

The Complete Life's Little Instruction Book

1281. Don't play your car stereo so loud that you can't hear approaching emergency vehicles.

1282. Take Trivial Pursuit cards to read to the driver on a long road trip. It makes the time fly.

1283. After children argue and have apologized, ask each one to say something nice about the other.

1284. Never forget the debt you owe to all those who have come before you.

1285. Memorize the names of the books of the Bible.

1286. Memorize the names and order of the Presidents.

1287. Remember that anything creative and innovative will be copied.

1288. Dress for the position you want, not the one you have.

1289. Don't write down anything you don't want someone else to read.

The Complete Life's Little Instruction Book

1290. Watch your back.

1291. Watch your weight.

1292. Watch your language.

1293. When traveling, pack more underwear and socks than you think you will need.

1294. When taking a true-false test, remember that any statement that includes the word *any, all, always, never*, or *ever* is usually false.

1295. Keep a couple of your favorite inspirational books by your bedside.

1296. Whisper in your sleeping child's ear, "I love you."

1297. At least once in your life, see the Grand Teton Mountains from the back of a horse.

1298. Let your children know that regardless of what happens, you'll always be there for them.

1299. Ask your boss what he expects of you.

1300. Never ignore a ringing fire alarm.

1301. Take a ride in a glider.

1302. Take a ride in a hot-air balloon.

1303. Be the first to apologize to a family member after a disagreement.

1304. To find out who is behind an idea or activity, follow the money.

1305. If you borrow something more than twice, buy one for yourself.

1306. When you build a home, make sure it has a screened-in porch.

1307. Be innovative.

1308. Be passionate.

1309. Be committed.

1310. Call a radio talk show with an opinion.

1311. Choose your life's mate carefully. From this one decision will come ninety percent of all your happiness or misery.

1312. During the winter months, keep a blanket in the trunk of your car for emergencies.

1313. Remember that life's most treasured moments often come unannounced.

1314. Don't get caught glancing at your watch when you're talking to someone.

1315. Never tell anybody they don't have a good sense of humor.

1316. Never tell anybody they can't sing.

1317. Don't argue with your mother.

1318. When deplaning, thank the captain for a safe and comfortable flight.

1319. Before buying that all-important engagement ring, find out all you can about diamonds by going to www.americangemsociety.org/ jewelrybuying.htm. The American Gem Society has information that will answer some of your questions.

1320. When parents introduce you to their children, say, "I have looked forward to meeting you, because your parents are always bragging about you."

1321. Every December, give the world a precious gift. Give a pint of blood.

1322. Plant a couple of fruit trees in your backyard.

1323. Wear a tie with cartoon characters on it if you work with kids.

1324. Remember that every age brings new opportunities.

1325. Know your children's friends.

1326. Eat lightly or not at all before giving a speech or making a presentation.

1327. Attend family reunions and be patient when aunts and uncles want to take your picture.

1328. Go for long, hand-holding walks with your wife.

1329. Visit the Biltmore estate in Asheville, North Carolina, during the spring tulip festival.

1330. Ask an older person you respect to tell you his or her proudest moment and greatest regret.

1331. Record the birthday heights of your children on the kitchen doorjamb. Never paint it.

1332. Every once in a while, let your kids play in the rain.

1333. Become the world's most thoughtful friend.

1334. Encourage exceptional students to become teachers.

1335. Always order bread pudding when it's on the menu.

1336. Create and maintain a peaceful home.

1337. When taking family photos, include a few routine, everyday shots.

1338. No matter how angry you get with your wife, never sleep apart.

1339. Never ask anyone why they wear a Medic Alert bracelet. That's his or her business.

1340. Tell gardeners of public areas how much you appreciate the beauty they bring to your city.

1341. Remember that anything worth doing is going to take longer than you think.

1342. Carry a kite in the trunk for windy spring days.

1343. Buy a flashlight for each person in your family to keep in their bedroom.

1344. Never marry someone in hope that they'll change later.

1345. Own a world globe.

1346. Own a good set of encyclopedias.

1347. Own a rhyming dictionary.

1348. Teach a Sunday school class.

1349. Find something that's important to your company and learn to do it better than anyone else.

1350. Don't eat anything covered with gravy unless you know what's under it.

1351. Don't eat anything covered with chocolate unless you know what's inside it.

1352. Keep a current city and state highway map in your car's glove box.

1353. Never call anybody stupid, even if you're kidding.

1354. When traveling, always pack a white dress shirt and a tie.

1355. Keep a photograph of each person you have dated.

1356. Be prudent.

1357. Be positive.

1358. Be polite.

1359. Don't drink anything blue.

1360. Buy your mom flowers and your dad a new tie with your first paycheck.

1361. Ever wonder what it takes to become an astronaut? Receive the application package by writing to Mail Code AHX, Johnson Space Center, Astronaut Selection Office, Houston, TX 77058-3696.

1362. Notify the manager when a restaurant's restroom isn't clean.

1363. Rebuild a broken relationship.

1364. When moving from a house or apartment, for nostalgia's sake, take a photo of each room while the furniture is still in place.

1365. Don't buy cheap picture frames.

1366. Don't buy a cheap tennis racket.

1367. Don't buy a cheap motorcycle helmet.

1368. Criticize the behavior, not the person.

1369. Never leave fun to find fun.

1370. Call three friends on Thanksgiving and tell them how thankful you are for their friendship.

1371. Collect seashells from your favorite beach.

1372. Collect menus from your favorite restaurants.

1373. Learn to make corn bread in a cast-iron skillet.

1374. Sniff an open bottle of suntan lotion and a fresh lime to temporarily curb the winter blues.

1375. Treat yourself to a professional shoeshine the next time you're at the airport.

1376. Ask your child to read a bedtime story to you for a change.

1377. Give a trusted auto technician all your repairs, not just the tough ones.

1378. Play Monopoly with your in-laws. It will reveal a lot about them.

1379. Write a letter of encouragement to the President—even if he didn't get your vote.

1380. Find a creative florist and give them all your business.

1381. Remember that when someone says, "You won't hurt my feelings. Tell me what you really think," they don't mean it.

1382. Send Valentines to your children as well as to your wife.

1383. When eating cinnamon rolls or prime rib, eat the center portion first.

1384. Add postscripts to your letters. Make them sweet and kind.

1385. Remember that bad luck as well as good luck seldom lasts long.

1386. Never let anyone challenge you to drive faster than you think is safe.

1387. Offer your place in line at the grocery checkout if the person behind you has only two or three items.

1388. When you see someone sitting alone on a bench, make it a point to speak to them.

1389. Keep receipts.

1390. Wet your hands before lifting a trout from the river.

1391. Don't force machinery.

1392. When walking a dog, let the dog pick the direction.

1393. Teach your children that when they divide something, the other person gets first pick of the two pieces.

1394. Stop at the visitor's information center when entering a state for the first time.

1395. When going to buy a car, leave your good watch at home.

1396. Never give a friend's or relative's name or phone number to a telephone solicitor.

1397. Put a love note in your wife's luggage before she leaves on a trip.

1398. Never buy an article of clothing thinking it will fit if you lose a couple of pounds.

1399. Don't be so open-minded that your brains fall out.

1400. Stand up when an elderly person enters the room.

1401. Root for your team to win, not for the other team to lose.

1402. This year, buy an extra box of Girl Scout cookies.

1403. Be grateful that God doesn't answer all your prayers.

1404. Accept triumph and defeat with equal grace.

1405. Exercise caution the first day you buy a chain saw. You'll be tempted to cut down everything in the neighborhood.

1406. Always watch the high school bands' halftime performances. They practiced just as hard as the football players.

1407. Never set a drink down on a book.

1408. Eat at a truck stop.

1409. Listen to your favorite music while working on your tax return.

1410. When a child is selling something for a dime, give a quarter.

1411. On long-distance road trips, make sure that someone besides the driver stays awake.

1412. Never give a pet as a surprise gift.

1413. Never ignore your car's oil warning light.

1414. After someone apologizes to you, don't lecture them.

1415. Make your wedding anniversary an all-day celebration.

1416. When you move into a new house, plant a rosebush and put out a new welcome mat to make it seem like home.

1417. Blow a kiss when driving away from loved ones.

1418. Carry a small Swiss Army knife on your key chain.

1419. Carry a couple of inexpensive umbrellas in your car that you can give to people caught in the rain.

1420. Never order barbecue in a restaurant where all the chairs match.

The Complete Life's Little Instruction Book

1421. When you complete a course, shake the instructor's hand and thank him or her.

1422. Contribute something to each Salvation Army kettle you pass during the holidays.

1423. Take more pictures of people than of places.

1424. Be willing to swap a temporary inconvenience for a permanent improvement.

1425. Learn and use the four-digit
extension to your ZIP code.

1426. Regarding rental property,
remember that an unrented
house is better than a bad tenant.

1427. When you really like someone,
tell them. Sometimes you only
get one chance.

1428. Never make fun of people who
speak broken English. It means
they know another language.

1429. When going through the checkout line, always ask the cashier how she's doing.

1430. When you need something done, ask a busy person.

1431. When traveling, carry the phone number and address of your destination in your wallet.

1432. Never underestimate the influence of the people you have allowed into your life.

1433. Read acknowledgments, introductions, and prefaces to books.

1434. Send a "thinking of you" card to a friend who's experiencing the anniversary of the loss of a loved one.

1435. Write a thank-you note to your children's teacher when you see your child learning new things.

1436. Learn your great-grandparents' names and what they did.

1437. Enter a room or meeting like you own the place.

1438. Refinish a piece of furniture at least once.

1439. Don't use your teeth to open things.

1440. Occasionally walk through old cemeteries and read the gravestones.

1441. When visitors ask, be able to recommend three or four free hometown "must sees."

1442. Never keep a free ride waiting.

1443. Share the remote control.

1444. If you ask someone to do something for you, let them do it their way.

1445. Once a year take your boss to lunch.

1446. Wave to train engineers.

1447. When visiting state and national parks, take advantage of all tours and lectures given by park rangers.

1448. Remember the best way to improve your kids is to improve your marriage.

1449. Call your parents as soon as you return from a long trip.

1450. Catch up on the bestsellers by listening to books on tape in your car.

1451 Learn to paddle a canoe.

1452. When someone you know is down and out, mail them a twenty-dollar bill anonymously.

1453. Savor every day.

1454. When pouring something from one container to another, do it over the sink.

1455. Aspirin is aspirin. Buy the least expensive brand.

1456. Never go up a ladder with just one nail.

1457. Protect your enthusiasm from the negativity of others.

1458. Remember, it never hurts to ask.

1459. If you live in the same city as your mother-in-law, occasionally trim her hedges and wash her car.

1460. Don't spend lots of time with couples who criticize each other.

1461. Ask yourself if what you're doing today is getting you closer to where you want to be tomorrow.

1462. Remember, it's not your job to get people to like you, it's your job to like people.

1463. Never buy a Rolex watch from someone who's out of breath.

1464. Never fry bacon while naked.

1465. Never squat with your spurs on.

1466. Pay attention to pictures of missing children.

1467. Read biographies of successful men and women.

1468. Offer to say grace at holiday meals.

1469. Bad things happen
in bad places,
so stay out of
bad places.

The Complete Life's Little Instruction Book

1470. When someone gives you a gift, never say, "You shouldn't have."

1471. Remember that the only dumb question is the one you wanted to ask but didn't.

1472. When you find a coin on the ground, pick it up and give it to the first person you see.

1473. Add *The Book of Virtues* by William Bennett (Simon & Schuster, 1993) to your home library.

1474. Never miss a chance to shake hands with Santa.

1475. Watch a video on CPR and emergency first aid with your family.

1476. Don't expect different results from the same behavior.

1477. Keep a couple of Wet-Naps in the glove box.

1478. Always offer guests something to eat or drink when they drop by.

1479. Spend time with lucky people.

1480. Wash whites separately.

1481. Never date anyone who has more than two cats.

1482. Make your bed every morning.

1483. Treat your parents to a dinner out on your birthday.

1484. When someone tells you they love you, never say, "No, you don't."

1485. Don't look through other people's medicine cabinets, closets, or refrigerators.

1486. When you race your kids, let them win at the end.

1487. For an unforgettable adventure, float the Gauley River in West Virginia.

1488. Remember that nothing important was ever achieved without someone's taking a chance.

1489. Once a summer, run through a yard sprinkler.

1490. Stand up for your high principles even if you have to stand alone.

1491. Watch reruns of *The Wonder Years.*

1492. When babies are born into your family, save the newspaper from that day. Give it to them on their eighteenth birthday.

1493. Hug a cow.

1494. Every couple of months, spend thirty minutes or so in a big toy store.

1495. Support family-run businesses.

1496. Carefully examine your written work when you are finished.

1497. Even on short ferry rides, always get out of your car and enjoy the crossing.

1498. Read *The Old Farmer's Almanac*.

1499. Never resist a generous impulse.

1500. When you are angry with someone, write a letter telling him or her why you feel that way—but don't mail it.

1501. When on vacation or a family holiday, don't be too concerned about the cost. This is not a time to count pennies; it's a time to make memories.

1502. Make sure the telephone number on your letterhead and business card is large enough to be read easily.

1503. Be faithful.

1504. Remember that everyone has bad days.

1505. Learn to eat with chopsticks.

1506. Never sharpen a boomerang.

1507. Never intentionally embarrass anyone.

1508. Question your prejudices.

1509. Be wary of stopping at restaurants displaying Help Wanted signs.

1510. Eat moderately.

1511. Exercise vigorously.

1512. When you're angry, take a thirty-minute walk; when you're really angry, chop some firewood.

1513. When returning a book or an item of clothing you have borrowed, leave a note of appreciation.

1514. Have your piano tuned every six months.

1515. When you pass a family riding in a big U-Haul truck, give them the "thumbs-up" sign. They need all the encouragement they can get.

1516 Avoid automated teller machines at night.

1517. Be the neighbor who always waves first.

1518. Watch what you eat at cocktail parties. Each hors d'oeuvre has about one hundred calories.

1519. Remember the main thing is to keep the main thing the main thing.

1520. Have your pastor over for dinner.

1521. Be sure the person you marry loves music.

1522. Take your family to a dude ranch for a vacation.

1523. Never break off communications with your children, no matter what they do.

1524. See any detour as an opportunity to experience new things.

1525. When adults are sick, care for them as though they were children.

1526. Clear your calculator after using it.

1527. Know when to leave a party. It's always five minutes before your hostess wants you to.

1528. Listen to rumors, but don't contribute any of your own.

1529. Learn the history of your hometown.

1530. Remember that wealth is not having all the money you want, but having all the money you need.

1531. Remember that much truth is spoken in jest.

1532. Say something every day that encourages your children.

1533. Remember that true happiness comes from virtuous living.

1534. Don't live with the brakes on.

1535. Visit the Art Institute of Chicago.

1536. Take a course in basic car repair.

1537. Never complain about the food or entertainment at church suppers or charity functions.

1538. When talking to someone who's a new parent, always ask to see a picture of the baby.

1539. If you know you're going to lose, do it with style.

1540. Use good stationery when you want your written comments to be taken seriously.

1541. Don't obligate yourself to a home mortgage larger than three times your family's annual income.

1542. When asked, take the time to give out-of-town visitors complete and clear directions.

1543. Never poke a snake with a short stick.

1544. Pass down family recipes.

1545. Don't forget that your attitude is just as important as the facts.

1546. Ask for advice when you need it, but remember that no one is an expert on your life.

1547. Rescue your dreams.

1548. Teach by example.

1549. Plant more flowers than you pick.

1550. Commit yourself to a mighty purpose.

1551. Remember that creating a successful marriage is like farming; you have to start over again every morning.

1552. Remember that all important truths are simple.

1553. Live simply.

1554. Think quickly.

1555. Work diligently.

1556. Fight fairly.

1557. Give generously.

1558. Laugh loudly.

1559. Love deeply.

1560. Include your parents in your prayers.

ACKNOWLEDGMENTS

I would like to thank the following contributors for sharing their advice and insights:

Christine Aitken, Lu Astrene, Donald Blackerby, Bernice Blake, Joseph J. Blank Jr., Heather Bledsoe, Brandy Blunden, Brad Brady, Jessica May Bridges, Blanche Broadbent, John R. Brubaker, Chris Burdette, Yvonne M. Burgess, Robert E. Burr, Nicole Burton, J. Bruce Camealy, H. Paul Canady III, Amanda B. Chambless, Sabrina Charles, Esther C. Chi, Timothy Cleavenger, Gary Cohen, Brenda Collins, Susan M. Condron, Lindsay Cook, LaShaunda Cox, Diane Crafts, Ovidin Cristea, Timothy Cundy, Jon Daniels, Megan E. Davis, Paul Davis, Mariken Hasert Deist, Tommy Doss, Julie Ann Dunaway, Pat Dygert, Kendall Eagan, Diane S. Emser, Joyce Evans, Maryhelen E. Evans, Carol Feneis, Charlene Fertig, Kari Lee Forde, Bonny L. Foster, Valerie Garfield, Marilyn Goodrich, Beth Grant, Josh Gray, Tobi Greer, Brandy Gregory, Kyra Harris, Matthew Hayhurst, Matthew J. Hire, Peggy Hope, Carole

L. Horn, Frederick F. Hovey Jr., Chandra Howard, Amy L. Huey, Sheryl Dickson Hunnie, Emma Jane Hunt, Brandy Jackson, Wendi Jackson, Lillian Jahngen, Reid Jason, Rebecca Ellen Johnson, Cliff Jones, Susan Kaschak, Patricia A. Kebles, Katie Kerlin, Hannah Kim, Chic Klinger, Ashley C. Knowles, Grace Kolek, Nick Kopsinis, Cheryl Kuelske, Daniele M. LaRoy, Anne Lavelle, Susan Lewis, Sari Litrach, Matt C. Little, Bethany Lombard, Samantha Loucks, Robyn Lowe, Mary Lynch, Kevin McAllister, Joan McConnel, Darin McCrea, Eileen McDermott-Pride, Kimberly A. McMunn, Terri Magrans, Matthew Makowicz, Maureen Malahovsky, Gina Malanga, Ryan Malone, Antonella Mangion, Lisa Marie Martello, Sheri Lyn Mayfield, Michael Mega, Jennifer Mendelis, Darlene Marie Miller, Jessica Lyn Miller, Martha A. Milhaem, Marie Milton, B. Omega Moore, Rick and Carmen Morgan, Cynthia Myers, Jane Nanbeck, Paula Nigro, Lori Nocito, Jeffrey A. Norton, Pat O'Brien, James D. O'Leary, David O'Malley, Irene Packard, Donna Diane Palmieri, Anna Lucille Parker, Julie S. Paschold, Christopher Peplinski, Dale W. Perry, Laurie Phelan, William Polvay, Donald D. Pruyn, Amy Quigley, Sharon Reinhardt, Brenda M. Ridgley, Ann Seidl

Rittal, Deborah L. Roye, Linda J. Rudman, James F. Rueber, Emma
Russell, Helen Russell, Raymond Sarin, Donna M. Schieber, Leslie
K. Schillinger, Mark Schymik, Mark W. Scott, Lana Shelstad, S. Todd
Shively, P. Willaim Simonini, Donna Sisco, Arona Smith, E.B. Starke,
R. Quintin Stephens, Adina L. Stone, Carrie Thomas, Diana Thomasian,
Esther Trumpower, Karen Utz, Elizabeth Pettit Varner, Grace Veloso,
Jana Washburn, Darrell Wayne, Joellen Welch, Carolyn D. Wells,
Douglas A. Welsh, Heidi Wengel, Mildred White, Teresa Whitehead,
Helen Alexander Williams, Dean E. Wilson III, Olivia Wong, Avaril
Woodward, Ruth H. Young, and Kelli Zenisek.

Dear Reader,

If you received advice from your parents or grandparents that was especially meaningful and would like for me to share it with other readers, please write and tell me about it.

I look forward to hearing from you.

H. Jackson Brown, Jr.
P.O. Box 150115
Nashville, TN 37215

www.instructionbook.com